𝒻RIENDSHIP BANDS

FRIENDSHIP BANDS

Braiding

Weaving

Knotting

Marlies Busch

Nadja Layer

Angelika Neeb

Elisabeth Walch

Sterling Publishing Co., Inc.
New York

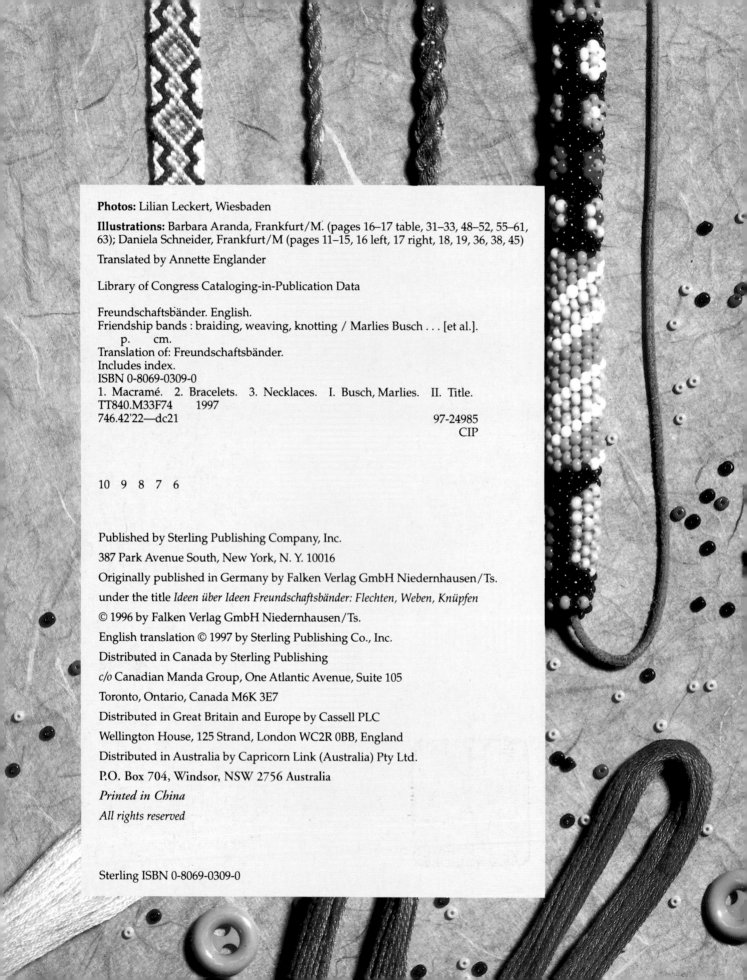

Photos: Lilian Leckert, Wiesbaden

Illustrations: Barbara Aranda, Frankfurt/M. (pages 16–17 table, 31–33, 48–52, 55–61, 63); Daniela Schneider, Frankfurt/M (pages 11–15, 16 left, 17 right, 18, 19, 36, 38, 45)

Translated by Annette Englander

Library of Congress Cataloging-in-Publication Data

Freundschaftsbänder. English.
Friendship bands : braiding, weaving, knotting / Marlies Busch . . . [et al.].
    p.   cm.
Translation of: Freundschaftsbänder.
Includes index.
ISBN 0-8069-0309-0
1. Macramé. 2. Bracelets. 3. Necklaces. I. Busch, Marlies. II. Title.
TT840.M33F74   1997
746.42'22—dc21
                                                97-24985
                                                  CIP

10 9 8 7 6

Published by Sterling Publishing Company, Inc.
387 Park Avenue South, New York, N. Y. 10016
Originally published in Germany by Falken Verlag GmbH Niedernhausen/Ts.
under the title *Ideen über Ideen Freundschaftsbänder: Flechten, Weben, Knüpfen*
© 1996 by Falken Verlag GmbH Niedernhausen/Ts.
English translation © 1997 by Sterling Publishing Co., Inc.
Distributed in Canada by Sterling Publishing
c/o Canadian Manda Group, One Atlantic Avenue, Suite 105
Toronto, Ontario, Canada M6K 3E7
Distributed in Great Britain and Europe by Cassell PLC
Wellington House, 125 Strand, London WC2R 0BB, England
Distributed in Australia by Capricorn Link (Australia) Pty Ltd.
P.O. Box 704, Windsor, NSW 2756 Australia
Printed in China

Sterling ISBN 0-8069-0309-0

CONTENTS

A FEW WORDS

When we put together this book, we wanted it to be full of wonderful ideas and stimulating projects. What we hopefully have is a rich sourcebook for everyone who enjoys making friendship bands and for those who want to learn how to. In it are not only the standard knotting techniques, but many others that can help you create enchanting bands.

Do you need a quick gift for a friend? No problem. Our projects are not only fun for the experienced bandmaker but they are also easy for beginners or people with little time. The bands in this book are not only meant to be bracelets. By coordinating colors and choosing the right material, many of them can be also used as necklaces, hair wraps, decorations on the zipper of backpacks and pencil cases, or on belt loops. You can even sew them onto your clothing, hang them on bulletin boards, or do many more things with them.

So now you can start! With the help of our examples and instructions, we hope that you'll make fantastic friendship bands—and maybe even be inspired to come up with new and creative ones on your own. We hope you have a lot of fun!

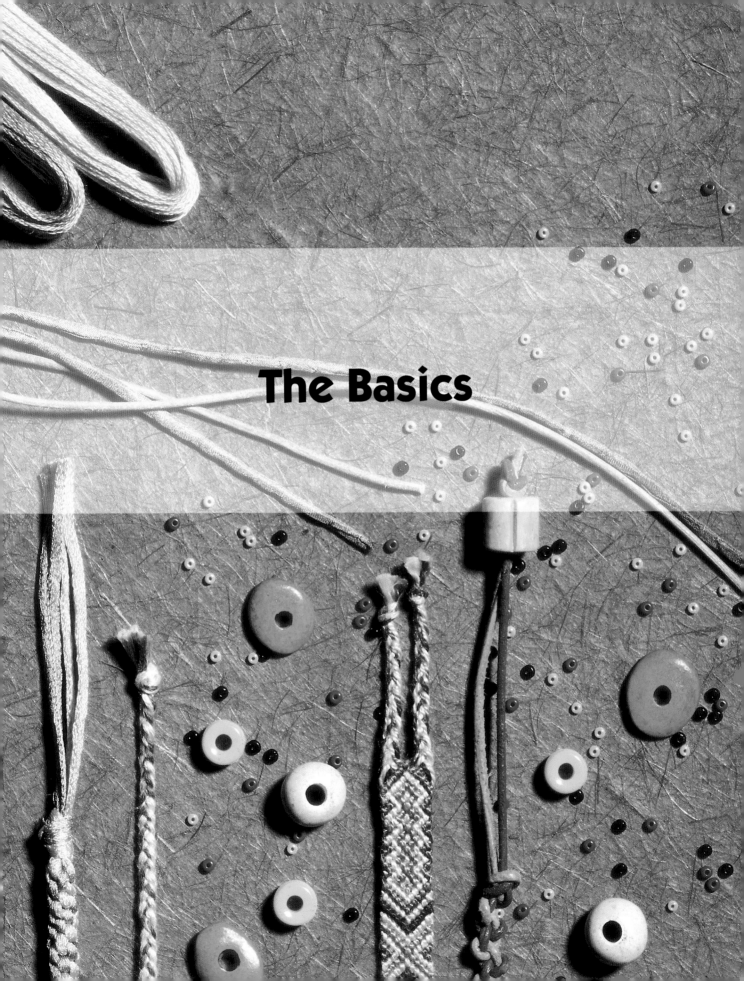

The Basics

TOOLS AND MATERIALS

Strings and Cords

The many different bands made in this book can vary depending on what the band will be used for. You have the choice of color, technique, and the type of material. In general, you should choose material that is not too frayed. Since the knots have to be drawn tightly, the thread also must not tear. **Embroidery floss** or **perle yarn** are ideal for fine-knotted friendship bands. Embroidery floss can be bought in infinitely varied colors and sometimes in different strengths. For coarser bands, such as those with macramé knots, you can use **silk strings** or **leather cords,** which are available in natural brown or are dyed. You can also, for a change, try out special needlework yarns, such as Lurex threads or narrow little knitted bands. Sewing thread is needed for fine beadworks, such as **transparent nylon thread** for when the threads are not supposed to be seen in stringed pieces. For bead-weaving pieces, a sturdy thread is good for the stretched warp; for the woof threads, you can also use a transparent nylon thread or a **colorful sewing thread.**

Beads

Some bead pieces in this book are made with **Native American beads.** When making a band, be sure that your beads are the same size so that there are no unwanted irregularities in the piece. Otherwise, you can decorate the bands with any kind of bead. Bead and craft stores offer a large variety of beads that are made of wood, ceramics, metal, glass, and many other materials in the most different shapes and colors. In choosing a bead, make sure that the opening is large enough for you to slip the thread through. Some of the bands in this book used colorful **buttons** as a clasp.

Supplies

You needs only a few tools to make a friendship band: a **tape measure** or **ruler,** a **pair of scissors,** and a **safety pin** or **adhesive tape.** For pieces that are made with beads, you need a thin, long **needle** that can go through the holes of the beads. For woven bands, you need a handy **bead loom** or **band-weaving loom.**

BASIC TECHNIQUES

Beginning and End

In order for the friendship band to be tied around the wrist, allow at least 4 inches of threads at both ends. Take one end of the knot (**Fig. a**) and attach it to a safety pin or with adhesive tape onto a textile surface. You can tie a strip of fabric around an armrest or the back of a chair to secure the safety pin or tape. To prevent the ends from fraying out, you can braid them, twist them into a cord, decorate them with a bead, or secure them with a knot. Little plaits look very nice.

If you want to have a loop at the end of the band, cut your threads twice as long as you need to work with, but cut only half as many threads. When you fold the threads in half, the number of threads you have will be multiplied by two.

Twisting Cords

Twisting the cord (**Fig. b**) is the most simple technique for an effective band. This is how it works:

- Based on how long you want the completed band to be, cut the threads at least three times longer. Fasten one end of the cord somewhere.
- Twist the cord in one direction (**Fig. b1**) until it becomes shorter and tighter and the first burl of the twist is visible.
- After you have twisted the cord, hold the middle of the cord with one hand. With the other hand, take the two ends together so that this double cord is now twisted together (**Fig. b2**).
- Secure the open end with a knot so that the cord stays together.

Winding Technique

This procedure creates round, colorful strings that can be worn not only around the wrist but also for tying your hair. The principle behind this technique is that different-colored threads are wrapped around a core of threads—or hair (**Fig. c**). The basic technique works this way:

- Cut threads of different colors about six times as long as the finished band. Fold the cord together to half the length.
- Leaving a loop on top, all the threads (and maybe a thin strand of hair) are tied together in a knot.
- Choose a thread for the first wrapping and wrap it tightly around all the other threads so that no color can be seen through this section (**Fig. c1**).
- When all the colors are covered, place the first thread finally into a loop and pull the end of the thread through into a tight knot (**Fig. c2**). Tuck this thread in with the others.
- Now continue to wrap around the cord with another piece of thread as described above. Then change to another thread.
- You can vary the technique so that you do not have only one-colored sections. For example, you can wrap another colored thread spirally around a completed section.
- Finally, secure the completed band with a knot and maybe decorate it with a bead.

Fig. a

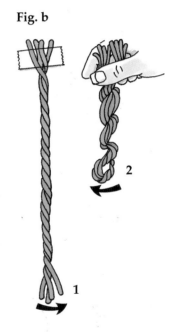

Fig. b

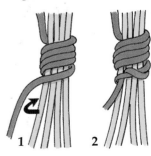

Fig. c

11

Fig. a

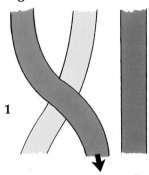

1

2

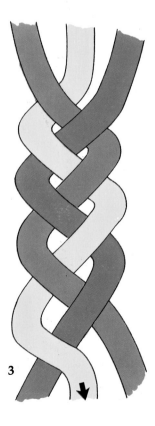

3

Braiding

Simple triple braid

Each strand consists of a single thread or string. If you use several threads grouped as a single strand, the braid becomes thicker **(Fig. a)**:

▷ Join the top of the three strands together with a knot. Fasten the knot to some surface and place the strands next to each other.

▷ First, fold the left strand *over* the next right one and leave it in the middle between the two other strands **(Fig. a1)**. Then place the far *right* one over to the middle **(Fig. a2)**. Do not braid too loosely.

▷ Continue alternating from both sides (from the *left* to the middle, from the *right* to the middle, from the *left* to the middle, and so on) until the braid is as long as you like **(Fig. a3)**.

▷ Secure the end with a knot.

Double braids

If you look closely, a double braid looks like two triple braids lying next to each other. You need seven strands for a double braid **(Fig. b)**:

▷ Join the top of the seven strands together with a knot. Fasten the knot on some surface and place the strands next to each other.

▷ Place the outer left strand *over* the next right one, then *under* the next *two* so that it ends up in the middle **(Fig. b1)**.

▷ Do the same thing with the outer *right* strand: fold it *over* the next left one, then *under* the next *two* so that it ends up in the middle **(Fig. b2)**.

▷ Continue alternating from both sides (from the *left* once over, twice under; then from the *right* once over, twice under; and so on) until the braid is as long as you like **(Fig. b3)**.

▷ Secure the end with a knot.

Ear braids

This braid got its name because it looks like the ears of a corn. The basic principle is always the same regardless of how many strands you braid with. Here is the instruction for eight strands with four colors **(Fig. c)**:

▷ Join the top of the eight strands together with a knot. Fasten it to a surface.

▷ Place the eight strands next to each other in such a way that the colors line up symmetrically on both sides. Starting from the middle, the colors look like a mirror image.

▷ First place the *left* outer strand *over* the right *three* strand so that it ends up in the middle **(Fig. c1)**.

▷ Then place the *right* strand (of the same color) over the four *left* ones so that it ends up in the middle. The strand of the same color is crossed over as well **(Fig. c2)**.

▷ Continue alternating from both sides (from the *left* over three, from the *right* over four, and so on) until the braid is long enough **(Fig. c3)**.

▷ Secure the end with a knot.

Woven braids

These braids are like woven fabric in the way that they are made. Here is the instruction for a triple braid with six strands **(Fig. d)**:

▷ Join the tops of the six strands together with a knot. Fasten it to a surface.

▷ First, place the outer *left* strand *over* the next right strand then *under* the following one so that two strands are crossed **(Fig. d1)**.

▷ Cross the outer *right* strand *under* the next left one, then *over* the following one and finally *under* the next one so that three strands are crossed **(Fig. d2)**.

- Continue alternating from both sides (from the *left* over, then under; from the *right* under, over, then under, and so on) until the braid is as long as you like **(Fig. d3)**.
- Secure the end with a knot.

Tip: Using four strands to make a woven braid is done similarly. Begin from the *left* over; then from the *right* under, over; from the *left* over; from the *right* under, over, and so on.

"Jewel in the Middle"

This braid is similar to the woven braids with four strands except that one color is left in the middle, decorating the braid like a "jewel." For this braid it is important to have three strands of the same color and one strand in a different, contrasting color. Here are the instructions **(Fig. e)**:

- Join the top of the four strands together with a knot. Fasten it to some surface.
- Place the four strands next to each other in such a way that two of the same color are on the left, the contrasting color strand follows, and next to it is the strand of the first color.
- First, lead the outer *left* strand over the next right one and *under* the following one **(Fig. e1)**.
- Then lead the outer *right* strand *under* the next left one and *over* the following one **(Fig. e2)**.
- Continue alternating from both sides (from the *left* over, under; from the *right* under, over; and so on) until the braid is as long as you like. If weaving is done correctly, the contrasting color will be straight in the middle of the braid **(Fig. e3)**.
- Secure the end-piece with a knot.

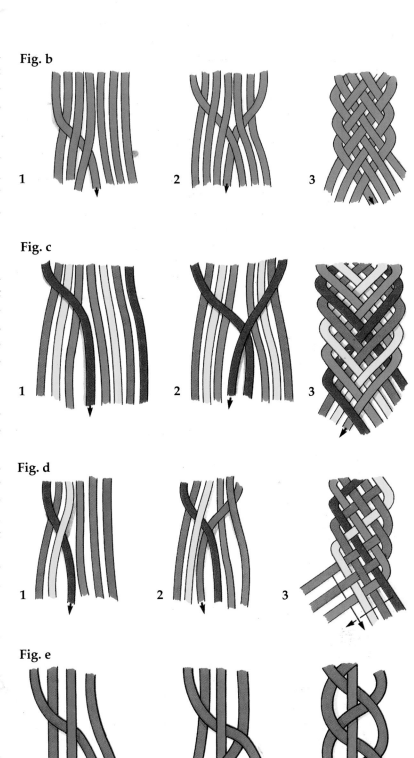

Fig. b 1 2 3

Fig. c 1 2 3

Fig. d 1 2 3

Fig. e 1 2 3

Fig. a

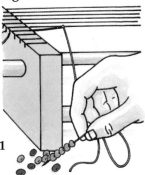

1

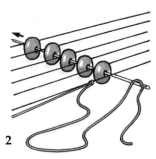

2

3

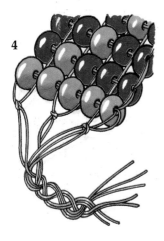

4

Weaving with Beads

Woven bands with beads may look complicated, but they are easy to make. You only need a bead loom (a small box or a picture frame will also do), sewing thread, small beads (generally, Native American beads), and a fine needle that fits through the holes of the beads and is longer than the band's width. Follow a counted pattern or create a design of your own by drawing a color sketch on checkered paper.

Stretching the warp thread

The number of the threads you use is based on the width of the desired band: If your band is to be eight beads wide, then nine warp threads are necessary. Use one more thread than the number of beads desired for the width. You can double the two outer threads to make the edge sturdier.

▷ Tie the beginning of the thread with a knot onto the loom.
▷ Stretch the threads parallel to each other on the loom (different models stretch the threads in a zigzag pattern or around the entire frame) so that the threads are long enough at both ends to tie around. The distance between the threads is the width of each bead.
▷ Finally, fasten the end of the threads to the frame.

Weaving

The threads that the beads will be weaved into are called warp threads (which run vertically in the design) and woof threads (which run horizontally). The color of the threads should either be transparent or coordinated with the basic color of the beads.

▷ Thread a piece of thread through a thin needle. Tie the end of the thread with a knot onto the frame and to the first warp thread.

▷ String the beads according to the pattern onto the needle **(Fig. a1)**, but not yet onto the thread, for the first row.
▷ Hold the needle with the row of beads *under* all of the warp threads transversely in such a way that the beads are resting exactly between the threads **(Fig. a2)**.
▷ Gently hold the beads in position with one finger while pulling the needle and thread through them. Do *not* let go of the beads.
▷ Now, from the other side, thread the needle through all beads but this time *over* the stretched warp threads **(Fig. a3)**. Again, do not let go of the beads while doing this.
▷ Pull the thread tightly and let go of the beads. They are now sitting firmly because the warp thread runs once above and below along the woof threads, thereby going through each bead twice. Weave all the other beads into the band in the same way by pushing each row carefully next to the previous one.

Finishing

▷ When the band is done, tie the woof thread onto the last warp thread with a knot.
▷ Cut off the warp threads so that the threads on both sides of the woven band are the same length.
▷ Tie these threads in pairs together with knots close to the beads so that nothing comes loose.
▷ You can either braid or twist the ends and secure them with knots **(Fig. a4)**.

Tip

▷ If your thread is about to run out while you are weaving, tie on a new thread and hide the knot and the ends of the thread inside the beads.

Round Strings Made of Beads

As opposed to the weaving process, where two threads (warp and woof) are being worked, there is only one continuous thread for stringing the beads in this technique. It is similar to sewing in some ways and the end result is a tubular band. A transparent sewing thread (nylon thread) is ideal for this technique. You also need small Native American beads, a fine sewing needle that fits through the holes of the beads, and a bit of patience.

Preparation

- Thread a fine needle with a nylon thread. Leave about 4 inches before tying a thick knot so that the beads cannot slip through.
- For a string in which each round has, for example, six or seven beads, you need a beginning round of thirteen beads. String these thirteen beads together and slip the needle and thread through the first bead so that the circle is closed (**Fig. b1**).

Stringing and making patterns

- The round of thirteen beads (shown in yellow in the figures) now becomes the first and second rows. The six beads in the first pattern round are shown in orange in the figures. The work is shown from a top view: Pass the threaded needle through one of the thirteen beads. Thread in a new bead and pass the needle through the third bead of the series (**Fig. b2**).
- Continue in this manner five more times in this round: string a new bead, pass the needle through the alternating bead, and so on. The alternating bead that is passed always sticks up a little so that you can easily recognize it.

- Begin a new round as the beads are shown in red in the figure. Continue the pattern of stringing and pass the needle as described above (**Fig. b3**), this time with seven beads. You will notice that the beads in each round are sitting in the gaps created by the previous round as shown if you opened up and laid flat the rounds (**Fig. b4**).
- Keep working in this manner by alternating six and seven beads for each round. It is not even necessary to count when you only concentrate on the colors of the chosen pattern.

Finishing

- When the round string is big enough, sew up the end and beginning threads. Cut off everything that is jutting out.
- Pull a sturdy string (for example, a leather cord) through the tube so that you could tie the ends of the string and have a wristband.

Tips

- If your thread is about to run out while you are weaving, tie on a new thread and try to hide the knot and the ends of the thread inside the tube after you're done.
- Having an uneven number of beads as your foundation round will give at many places a starting point for a pattern. If you want to prevent this by having an even number of beads, the technique becomes more complicated because you would have to finish each new round into a bead. That, unfortunately, is hardly possible without having to count. Your work will go much more quickly with an uneven number of beads as your foundation round.

Fig. b

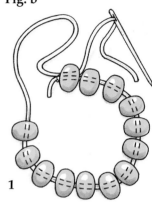

1

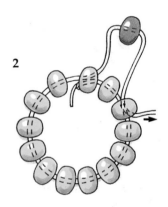

2

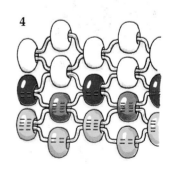

3

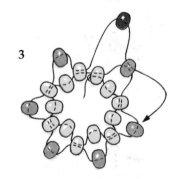

4

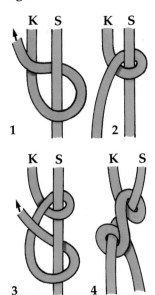

Basic Knots

The most popular knot for friendship bands is often the basic knot that is made with two threads and which is basically a double knot. It can be knotted in both directions. One thread forms the knot (k) while the other bears the knot or stands to be knotted (s).

Basic knot, clockwise

▶ Place the knotting thread from the left over the standing thread and curl it around. Pull the knot tight and place the knotting back to the left. Pull the knot tight **(Figs. a1–2)**.

▶ Curl the knotting thread again around the standing thread. Pull it tight and now place it to the right **(Figs. a3–4)**.

▶ The completed knot appears in the color of the knotted thread, which runs from the left to the right.

Basic knot, counterclockwise

▶ This time, place the knotting thread from the right over the standing thread and curl it around. Pull the knot tight and place the knotting thread back to the right **(Figs. b1–2)**.

▶ Curl the knotting thread again around the standing thread. Pull it tight and now place it to the left **(Figs. b3–4)**.

▶ The completed knot again appears in the color of the knotted thread, which this time runs from the right to the left.

Fig. b

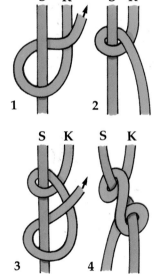

Name of the knot	Diagram of the course ıfs of the thread	Symbol in the patterns (p. 48 ff)
Basic knot, clockwise	K S S K	▶●
Basic knot, counterclockwise	S K K S	◀●

The arrow of the symbol depicts the active knotting thread (k) in the respective color, the dot the passive standing thread (s).

The row of the vertical color lines shows the sequence that the threads have to lie in after the last step: ▮▮ ▮ ▮ ▮ ▮ ▮ ▮

All the steps are depicted in straight rows, but in general they run diagonally.

Double Half-hitch Knots

The knotting thread (k) in the basic knots always runs in *one* direction through the knot, but it changes direction in the double half-hitch knot. The double half-hitch knot can also be worked clockwise or counterclockwise.

Double half-hitch knot, counterclockwise

▹ As in the basic knot, place the knotting thread from the left over the standing thread and curl it around. Pull the knot tight to the left **(Fig. c1)**.

▹ Then alternate the knotting thread to the right **(Fig. c2)**.

▹ Curl the knotting thread from the right around the standing thread. Pull it tight and then place it again to the left **(Fig. c3)**.

▹ The finished knot appears in the color of the knotting thread **(Fig. c4)**.

Double half-hitch knot, clockwise

▹ Place the knotting thread from the right over the standing thread and curl it around. Pull the knot tight towards the right **(Fig. d1)**.

▹ Then alternate the knotting thread to the left **(Fig. d2)**.

▹ Now curl the knotting thread from the left around the standing thread. Pull it tight and then place it again to the right **(Fig. d3)**.

▹ The completed knot appears in the color of the knotting thread **(Fig. d4)**.

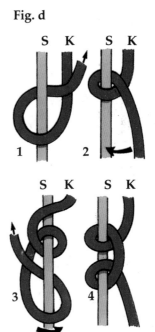

Fig. c

Fig. d

Name of the knot	Diagram of the course of the threads	Symbol in the patterns (p. 48ff)
Double half-hitch knot, counterclockwise	K S K S	◉
Double half-hitch knot, clockwise	S K S K	◈

Y and ✕ mean: two threads of the same color are tied together (basic or half-hitch knot).

Sequence:

▹ If symbols and arrows point to the Y, e.g., ❯Y❮ the outer knots are first tied and then the threads in the middle are tied together.

▹ If symbols and arrows point away from the ✕, e.g., ◉✕◈, the threads in the middle are first tied together and then the outer knots are tied.

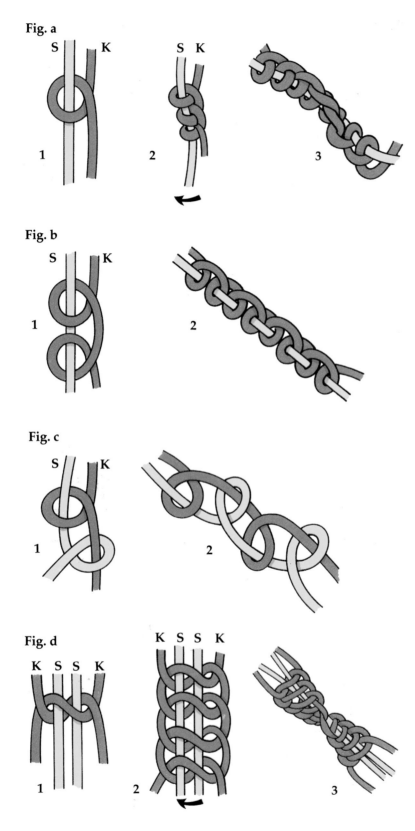

Fig. a

Fig. b

Fig. c

Fig. d

Macramé

The following knots present a small selection from traditional macramé. They are needed for the instructions in the main part of this book.

Half-hitch knot

The half-hitch knot is one of the most basic macramé knots. It is part of the basic and double half-hitch knots mentioned in pages 16–17: The knotting thread (k) is curled once around the standing thread (s) and then pulled tightly (**Fig. a1**). Many half-hitch knots and their variations are knotted in the same way to form a spiral. The standing and knotting threads always remain the same (**Figs. a2–3**).

Double half-hitch knot

The double half-hitch knot (page 17) is also the same as a clove hitch knot. It consists of two half-hitch knots that are knotted in opposite directions (**Fig. b1**). You can make a long string with it that does *not* (as in the case of the simple half-hitch knot) twist into a spiral. The standing and knotting threads remain always the same (**Fig. b2**).

Half-hitch chain knot

The half-hitch chain knot is also created with the half-hitch knot except, after each knot, the knotting and the standing threads exchange roles. This leaves no "spine" in the knot (**Figs. c1–2**).

Half knot

For the classic half knot, two standing threads are lying passively in the middle while the two knotting threads always curl around them (**Figs. d1–2**).

By making a series of these half knots, you can create a spiral (**Fig. d3**).

Square Knot

The square (or flat) knot, a very popular macramé knot, consists of two half knots that are knotted alternately. For example, the knotting thread, which is coming from the *left*, is lead once *over* the standing threads and then the knotting thread, which is coming from the *right* (**Figs. e1–2**). Making a series of square knots creates a flat band that does not twist (**Fig. e3**).

Fig. e

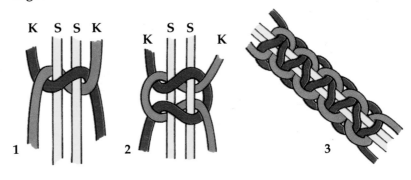

Monk's cord

The name of this cord supposedly stems from the cloisters in which the monks made binding belts for their cowls. This technique creates a round, quite elastic cord. This is how it works:

Fig. f

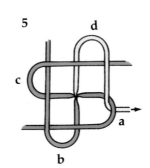

- ▶ Tie four threads together with a knot. Hold the knot.
- ▶ Place the threads in four directions (**Fig. f1**).
- ▶ Choose a thread at the beginning of the round. Place that thread clockwise over only *one* adjacent thread, as shown in thread *a* over thread *b* (**Fig. f2**).
- ▶ Then lead thread *b* in the same direction over the next *two* threads, as shown in threads *a* and *c* (**Fig. f3**).
- ▶ Follow by placing thread *c* in the same direction over the *two* next threads, *b* and *d* (**Fig. f4**).
- ▶ At the end of the round, lead thread *d* over threads *c* and *a*. Then loop thread *d* under thread *a* (**Fig. f5**).
- ▶ Pull all threads tight and the first round is finished (**Fig. f6**).
- ▶ Begin the next round with any thread. Weave as described above: Lead the four threads one after another *once* over *one* thread and *three times* over *two* threads and loop in under the first thread. Always weave in the same direction.

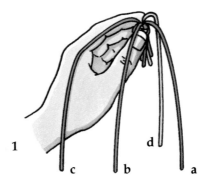

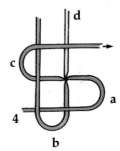

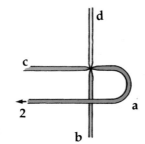

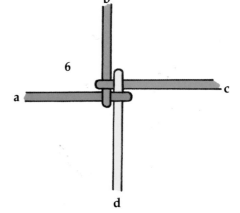

Various Bands

Quickly Twisted Cords

These friendship bands, finished with a bead twist, are created at lightning speed. Add some unique beads at the end and you have a small gift for your best friend.

Instructions

Different-colored Bands

- As shown in the six lower bands in the photo on the left, choose strings whose colors go together. For example: blue and green, red and yellow, lilac and pink.

- Cut several threads that are 20 inches long and place them together. For a thin cord use at least three threads; there are no limits for the maximum number you can use.

- Fasten the threads at one side and then twist them in one direction until they become tight and short (see also basic techniques on page 11).

- Then hold the strand in the middle and bring both of the ends together. The cord will twist together by itself. Tie a knot about 2¾ inches away from the end to stop it from unraveling.

- The free ends can be finished completely to your liking. It is best to divide the strands so that you can braid them (see pages 12–13), decorate them with beautiful beads, and secure the ends with a knot.

Two-colored Bands

- The two upper bands in the photo on the left are examples of two-colored cords. You need the same number of threads for each color. Cut off 20 inches for each thread.

- Tie the two thread groups (for example, one red and one blue) together in such a way that 2¾ inches hang freely.

- Divide the threads according to their color. Fasten only the free ends of *one* thread group (for example, the red threads) with adhesive tape onto a surface.

- Take the ends of the threads with the different colors into your hand so that the beginning knot is in the middle.

- Now twist the entire strand like it is done for a normal cord.

- Hold the knot in the middle, bring the two ends with different colors together, and tie them together with a knot about 2¾ inches away from the end. Check the length against your wrist beforehand.

- Create the ends to your liking. It looks nice when you divide them by color and make two braids.

WHAT YOU NEED:
- Embroidery floss and Lurex threads
- Matching beads
- Pair of scissors and measuring tape
- Adhesive tape or safety pin

Colorful Braids

Braiding is probably one of the most simple ways of creating a pretty friendship band. Using beautiful colors and unusual materials, you can quickly and easily make an exquisite piece of jewelry.

Instructions

Triple Braid

- For the simple braid (on the bottom of photo), cut three silk strings of different colors to about 18 inches long and place them together.
- Leave on top about 4¾ inches free, then tie the three strings together with a knot and fasten this knot onto a surface.
- Now braid it into a simple triple braid (see page 12) until the band is long enough. Finally, tie the strings together again.
- Make a simple knot at the end of the individual strings.

Colorful Double Braid

- Choose seven threads to make the braid in the middle of the photo. From each of those, cut two threads to a length of about 16 inches. Place all the threads together.
- Leave on top 4 inches free, then tie all threads together with a knot. Fasten this beginning piece to a surface.
- Arrange the threads next to each other in such a way that the two threads of the same color create a common strand. The colors of the band in the photo are: red, orange, yellow, violet, blue, medium green, and dark green.
- Following the instruction on page 12, make your double braid the desired length, then finish the braid with a knot.
- To complete the braid, decorate both ends with triple braids and then secure with a knot.

Yellow Double Braid

- To make the yellow braid on top of the photo, cut each of these threads to about 16 inches: four in yellow, four in orange, four in light green, and two in dark green.
- After the beginning piece has been secured as described above, place the threads (each time using two of the same color together) in the following symmetrical sequence next to each other: yellow, orange, light green, dark green, light green, orange, yellow.
- Braid the double braid as described on page 12 to the length you want. Decorate the ends with triple braids and secure with a knot.

WHAT YOU NEED:
- Embroidery floss or silk strings in different colors
- Pair of scissors and measuring tape
- Adhesive tape or safety pin

Braid Variations

Whether it is an ear braid or a "jewel in the middle" braid, these styles of braiding are fun to make and beautifully colorful.

Instructions

"Jewel in the Middle"

- To make the braid on top of the photo, you need four strands that are about 20 inches long. In the photo, three embroidery flosses are in violet and one is in blue.
- Fold the threads in half so that you have a little loop on top and then make a knot. Arrange the threads in such a way that always two of the same color form a strand. The sequence from left to right is: violet, violet, blue, violet.
- Braid the "jewel in the middle" (according to the instructions on page 13) until the band is long enough.
- Secure the braid with a knot and braid the ends with two simple triple braids.

Woven Braids with Leather Strings

- To make the braid in the photo that is second from the top, fold in half three leather strings of different colors. Leave a loop on the top, wind one of the strings around it, and fasten it with a knot.
- Fasten this beginning piece to a surface.
- Place the colors of the six strands next to each other symmetrically. For example, the strands of the band in the photo are placed in this sequence: green, Bordeaux, blue, blue, Bordeaux, green.

- Follow the woven braid instructions on pages 12–13 to complete the braid. Secure the end with a knot.

Quadruple Braid

- The third braid in the photo needs four strands as well. These strands consist of two embroidery floss threads each.
- Braid according to the instructions for woven braids on pages 12–13.

Ear Braids

- For the two ear braids at the bottom of the photo, cut eight strands of embroidery floss about 22 inches long. The eight strands consist of four colors. Fold them in half.
- Form a loop at the top and secure it with a knot. Fasten it to a surface.
- Place the sixteen strands in symmetrical sequence next to each other, here: green, yellow, red, orange, orange, red, yellow, green. Each color consists of two strands.
- Following the instructions on page 12, make an ear braid of the desired length and secure it with a knot.
- Divide the ends and braid them with little triple braids.

TIP: The yellow-green ear braid in the photo is a variation made of seven strands.

28

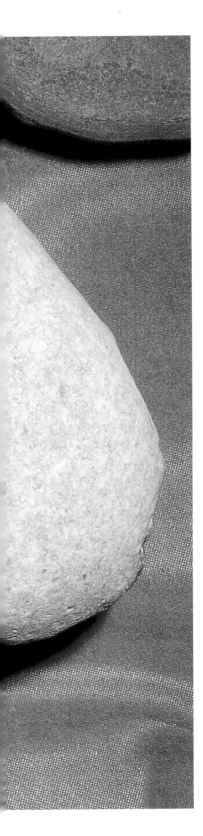

Monk's Cord

The monks in early times knew how to make an elastic binding belt for their cowls. These friendship bands employ the same simple technique. The beginning piece of these bands is not, as for the other braided bands, fastened with a safety pin or adhesive somewhere. Instead, you hold the end of the threads with one hand while the other hand weaves the threads over each other.

Instructions

Speckled Cord

- To make the far left cord in the photo, choose three silk strings of one color and a fourth string of a contrasting color.
- Leave at the beginning about 4 inches free before you hold the four strings together with a knot.
- Hold on to the knot between your thumb and forefinger so that the free ends are hanging down from inside your hand (see **Fig. f** on page 19). Look down onto the knot to be sure that the four working threads are pointing in all four directions.
- Follow the instructions on page 19 to make the monk's cord. Pull the threads evenly after each row. Weave the threads in the same direction. It does not matter with which thread you begin the next round.
- When the cord is long enough, tie a knot at the end to prevent it from unraveling.
- Tie a knot also on the free ends.

Spiral Cord

- For this cord in the middle of the photo, tie two blue and two yellow silk bands together with a knot. At the beginning of the first round, make sure that the two bands of the same color are lying opposite each other.
- Make the monk's cord as described above and according to the instructions on page 19. The two colors create a spiral-shaped pattern.
- When the cord is long enough, secure the ends with a knot.

Four-colored Cord

- For the monk's cord on the right photo, combine in four colors perle yarn or viscose yarn.
- Make the monk's cord as described above according to the instructions on page 19. When it is long enough, secure the ends with knots.

WHAT YOU NEED:

- Native American beads
- Sewing or buttonhole thread
- Nylon thread
- Fine sewing needle or bead needle
- Bead loom
- Pair of scissors and measuring tape

Spectacular Bead Bands

These bands, full of contrast, can be easily made with thread and Indian beads, which can be bought in many colors. Wouldn't one of these bands be a great personalized gift for a dear friend?

Instructions

Yellow Bead Band

▶ To make the yellow band in the photo, stretch eight warp threads (made of black buttonhole threads) onto the bead loom, because it is seven beads wide (see page 14).

▶ To begin weaving, you need yellow, black, and red Native American beads as well as nylon thread. Follow the pattern row by row in **Figure a**. String the beads onto the thin needle and weave them into the stretched warp threads according to the instructions on page 14. Repeat the motif between the arrows as often as you need until your band is long enough.

▶ Finally, remove the warp threads from the frame, secure the first and last bead rows with several knots, and braid the threads together (see instructions on page 14).

Wide Zigzag Pattern

▶ To make this band on the left of the photo, you need Native American beads in only two colors and eight warp threads. Work the band according to the pattern in **Figure b** and the instructions on page 14.

▶ Complete the finished band as described above.

Checkered Band

▶ You need only black and white Native American beads for this band, whose pattern is very similar to the yellow bead band. Stretch eight warp threads onto the bead loom and work the band according to the pattern in **Figure c** and the instructions on page 14. Repeat the motif between the arrows as often as you like until your band is long enough.

▶ Complete the finished woven band as described above.

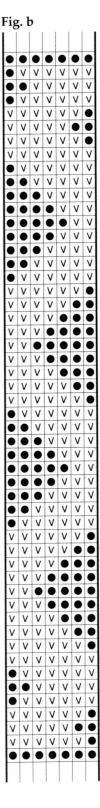

Fig. a **Fig. c**

○ Yellow

● Black

✳ Red

v White

Multicolored Bead Bands

The color choices suggested in these patterns are partly strong, partly subtle. Of course, you can always substitute any of these colors with your own favorites.

Fig. a

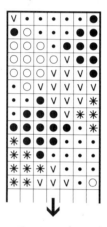

- •   Yellow   v   Green
- ○   Blue   ✳   Red
- ●   Black

Fig. b

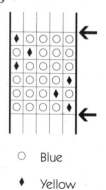

- ○   Blue
- ◆   Yellow

Instructions

Colorful Checkered Band

▷ To make the band at the top of the photo, stretch eight warp threads (made of black threads) onto the bead loom because it is seven beads wide (see page 14).

▷ To begin weaving, you need beads in at least five colors. Follow the pattern in **Figure a** according to the instructions on page 14. You can substitute our color suggestions with ones of your choice.

▷ The arrow at the bottom of the pattern means that the pattern can be repeated from that point on as often as you like until the band is long enough.

▷ Remove the warp threads from the loom, secure the first and last bead rows with several knots, and braid the threads together (see instructions on page 14).

Blue and Yellow Band

▷ To make this band, you need Native American beads in only two colors and six warp threads because it is only five beads wide. Make the band following the pattern in **Figure b** and the instructions on page 14. Repeat the motif between the arrow points as often as necessary until the band is long enough.

▷ Complete the finished woven band as described above.

Native American Band

▸ To make the third band in the photo (which shows a pattern of the Winnebago Indians) you need beads in four colors and eight warp threads. Make the band following the pattern in **Figure c** and the instructions on page 14. Weave the motif between the arrow-points as often as you like.

▸ Complete the band as described for the other bands on page 32.

Fine Stripes Band

▸ The band on the bottom of the photo is five beads wide, so that you must stretch six warp threads.

▸ Beside the white beads, you can use the leftover beads from other bands. Make the band with the colors of your choice according to the pattern in **Figure d** and the instructions on page 14.

▸ Weave the motif between the arrow-points as often as you like until the band is long enough.

▸ Complete the band as described for the other bands on page 32.

- White

○ Blue

■ Orange

✻ Red

WHAT YOU NEED:
- Native American beads
- Sewing or buttonhole threads
- Nylon thread
- Fine sewing or bead needle
- Pair of scissors and measuring tape

Fig. c

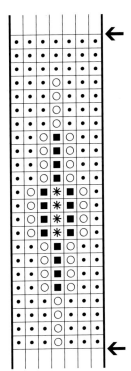

Fig. d

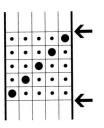

- White

● Any color scheme

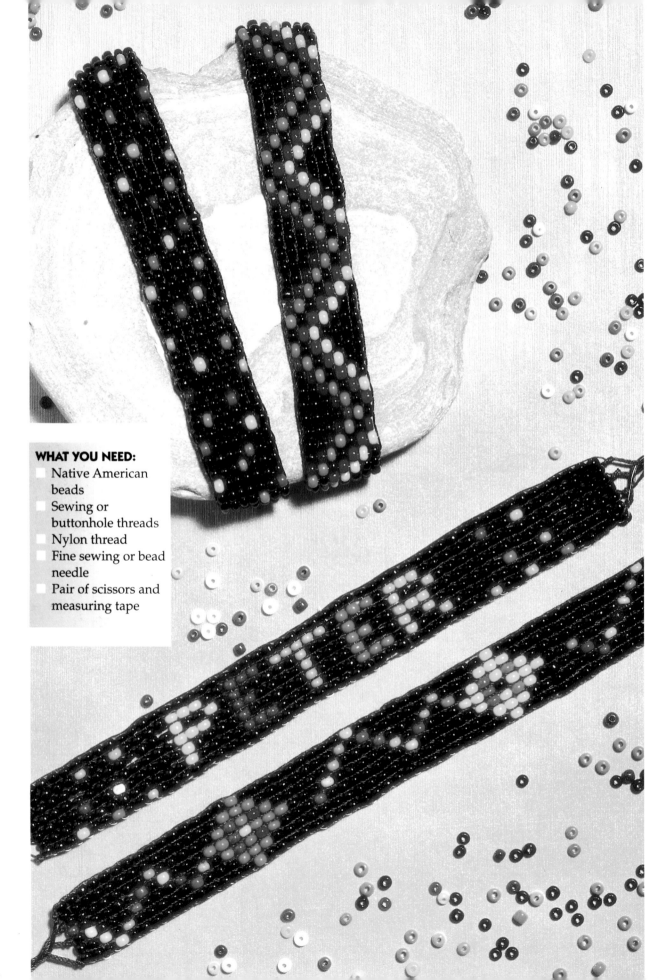

WHAT YOU NEED:
- Native American beads
- Sewing or buttonhole threads
- Nylon thread
- Fine sewing or bead needle
- Pair of scissors and measuring tape

Black Bands with Color Spots

Different colors on a black surface always have an eye-catching effect. Finding the right pattern can give the band either an elegant or a playful feel.

Instructions

Little Dots

- Stretch eight black warp threads for the top left band in the photo, which is seven beads wide.
- Weave the band according to the instructions on page 14. Use black beads and intersperse colored beads to your liking.
- Complete the band as described for the other bands on page 32.

Fig. b

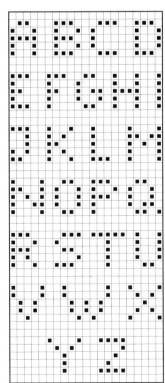

Fine Zigzag Pattern

- Stretch eight black warp threads for the top right band in the photo, which is seven beads wide. Work according to the pattern in **Figure a** and the instructions on page 14. Use beads in black and four other colors.
- The arrows indicate the beginning and end of the motif, which can be repeated until the band is long enough. Finish as described above on page 32.

Name Band

- Using the alphabet pattern in **Figure b**, anyone can design a first name or initials on a band.
- You need eight warp threads because the band will be seven beads wide (each letter is five beads high). Follow the instructions on page 14 to make the band and complete it with braids.

Dragon Band

- You need eight warp threads because the band will be seven beads wide.
- Weave the beads following the instructions on page 14. Use black and as many colorful beads as you like. Complete the pattern in **Figure c** according to your own ideas and finish the band as described above.

Fig. a

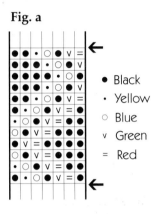

- ● Black
- · Yellow
- ○ Blue
- v Green
- = Red

Fig. c

- ● Background
- · Dragon's face
- * Dragon's eyes
- ■ Dragon's nose
- ▯ Dragon's mouth
- ○ Dragon's tail

Blossom Chains

These delicate-looking blossom chains are not only ideal for wearing on your wrist, but they also look great as necklaces.

Fig. a

1

2

3

Instructions

Chain in Rainbow Colors

- Cut a nylon thread about 48 inches long and thread it into the needle. Make a thick knot about 4 inches away from the end of the thread.
- For the first blossom, string eight Native American beads of the same color, then thread the needle back through the first bead **(Fig. a1)**.
- For the center of the blossom, string one bead of another color, jump over four beads in the row, and thread into the fifth bead **(Fig. a2)**. Pull the thread tight and the first blossom is made.
- String two black beads before starting the next blossom.
- Then begin stringing the next blossom using another color combination **(Fig. a3)**.
- Continue the chain in this way until it is long enough. Finally, sew up the end to the beginning.

Colorful Friendship Band

- Sew a button that will match the color of your blossom band onto a nylon thread.
- Make a short chain, as described before, but leave out the black connecting beads between the blossoms.
- When it is long enough for your wrist, make a loop by stringing as many beads as you need and then closing the beads to make a ring. This way, you have a clasp for the button.

Black and White Band

- This friendship band is made in the same way as the two previous ones except that you use white beads for the blossoms and eight black beads to connect them.
- Complete the band as described before.

Blue Band

- For this variation, use only beads of three colors. Choose one color for the outside of the blossom, another for the inside, and another for connecting them.
- When the band is sufficiently long, finish it as described before.

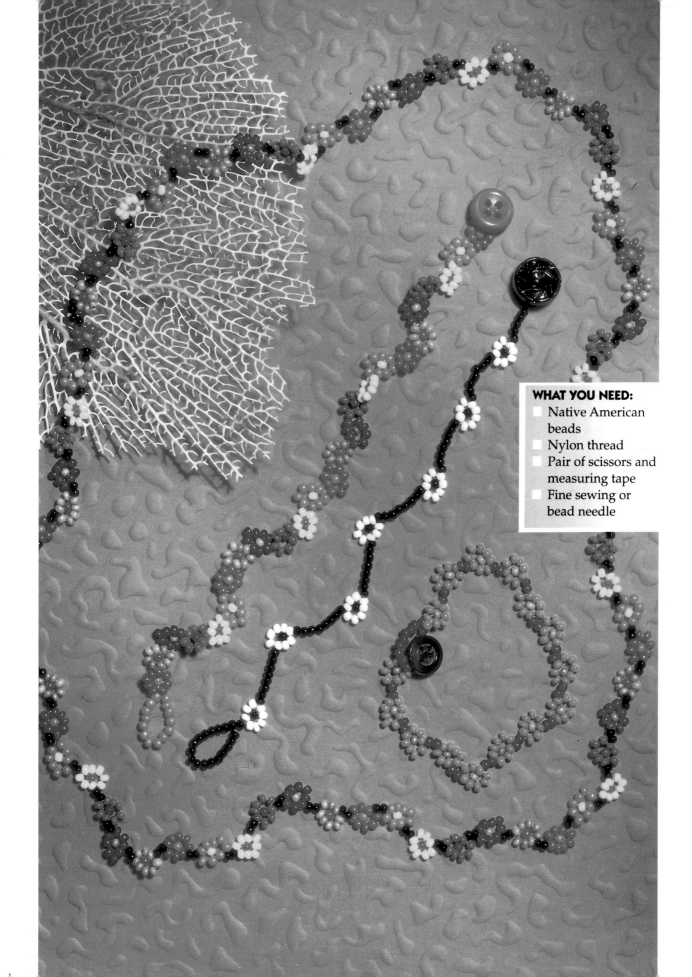

WHAT YOU NEED:
- ☐ Native American beads
- ☐ Nylon thread
- ☐ Pair of scissors and measuring tape
- ☐ Fine sewing or bead needle

Decorative Bead Strings

An old technique is coming alive again: stringing bead by bead so that you create interesting patterns out of the rows, which lie above one another in a spiral.

Instructions

Flower Band

- Thread the nylon thread into a needle and make a thick knot about 4 inches away from the end so that no bead can slide off.
- String thirteen black beads and then thread the needle back into the first bead so that the circle is closed.
- Continue working each round as described in the instructions on page 15. The pattern in **Figure a** shows what the band looks like if it was opened up and laid flat. String a yellow bead in the first pattern row between each black bead three times.
- In the second row, string six yellow beads and then one black bead as a transition to the next round. One black bead separates the yellow ones, except in one area (where there are two black beads).
- In the third row, follow the colors of the previous round, except place a green bead into each yellow "triangle."
- Create the fourth round like the second round by using only yellow beads.
- "Close" the flower in the fifth round with three yellow beads, like the first round.
- Now work four rounds of black beads before starting the next flower pattern.
- Continue this way until the string is long enough.
- Tie a knot into the end pieces of the thread and sew them up. Pull a leather cord through the hollow tube of the band. Now this friendship band can be easily tied around your wrist.

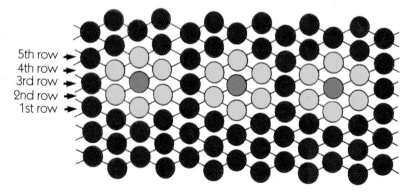

5th row →
4th row →
3rd row →
2nd row →
1st row →

Fancy-colored Band

▸ To make the multicolored band in the photo, string thirteen orange beads and work two rounds of it following the instructions on page 15. Then create the patterns as shown in the photo (from the bottom upward).

▸ *Black spiral in orange:* Place only one black bead into the first round. Add again only one black bead in the following round so that it is one bead in front of the black bead of the previous round. This way, a spiral "grows."

▸ *Black ring:* Make the three rows with black beads.

▸ *Red and white surface:* First, work several red rows, then begin at one spot with *one* white bead. Add in the following round *two* white beads exactly above the one in the previous round. In the next row, add *three* and so on until only white beads fill the round.

▸ *Green lattice of lines:* Add in the first black row one green bead. In the next row, add before and after the green bead of the first row one more green bead to the side of it. After that, continue adding beads in each round to create two slanted lines that go around and eventually intersect.

▸ *Fine rings:* The red section is interrupted by horizontal dotted lines. To do that, create a round in a contrasting color.

▸ When the band is long enough, complete it as described on page 38.

WHAT YOU NEED:
- Native American beads
- Nylon thread
- Pair of scissors and measuring tape
- Fine sewing or bead needle

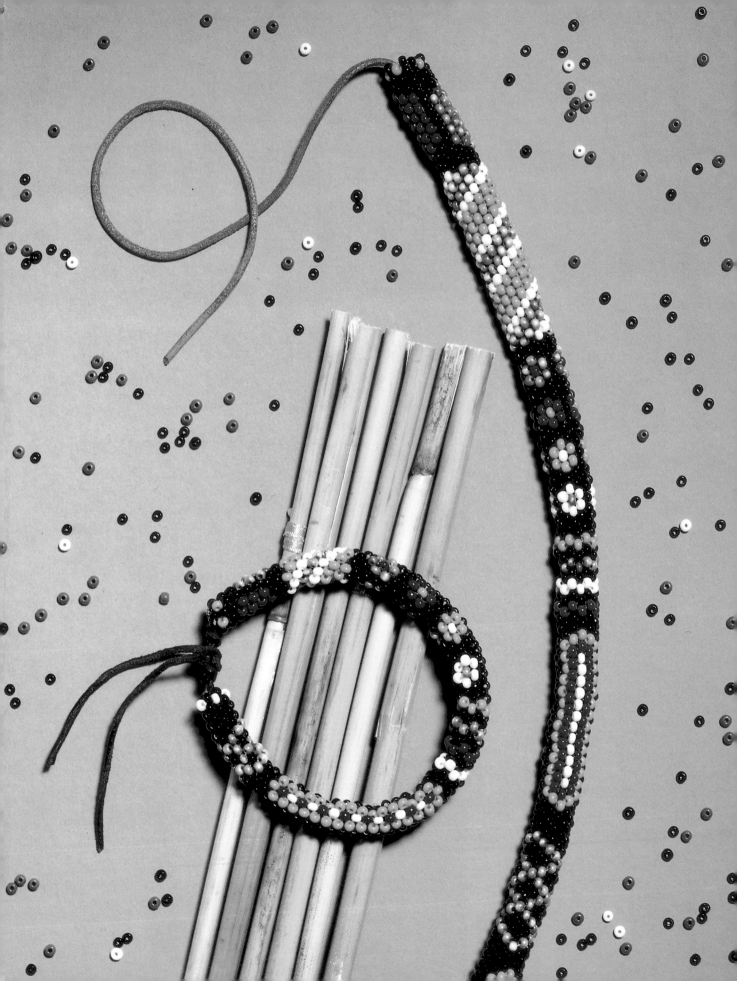

Patterns in Blue

A lot of patterns for a bead string can be developed by experimenting. White, pink, blue, and green beads are complementary in color and they stand out well against a black background.

Instructions

Chain

▶ Begin with a round of thirteen black beads following the instructions on page 15. The background color will be black. Here are some of the patterns seen in the bands in the photo.

▶ *Pink and blue stripes:* On opposite sides of the first round, add one blue and one pink bead. In the following rounds, add two, then three beads of each color above their respective beads from the previous round. Then reduce the number of blue and pink beads by one in the subsequent rounds so that you end up with triangles.

▶ *Spiral:* After several black rounds, string *one* pink bead, *one* white bead, *three* green beads, and *one* white bead.

▶ Then open the next round with *two* pink beads and then, as before, one white bead, three green beads, and one white bead. Repeat the colors in the following rounds so that they shift in this way until you get a multicolored spiral.

▶ *Flowers:* These are worked according to the instructions on page 38 except, here, we use different colors and there is less distance in rows between the flowers.

▶ *Rings:* These can be created by alternating two rounds of a different-colored bead with two rounds of black beads.

▶ *Multicolored stripes:* These are made like the pink and blue stripes previously described, except that you use three colors.

▶ *Pink lattice lines:* On the opposite sides of the first round, add a pink bead. In the following round, place at these two spots one bead *before* and *after* them. In the next round, again add four beads following the direction of before and after, so that you get four slanted lines that eventually intersect.

▶ From that point, create the pattern in reversed sequence and complete the band as described in the instructions on page 15. Finally, pull a leather cord through the bead tube. Now you can tie it around your wrist or, if it is long enough, around your neck.

Friendship Band

▶ To make a matching friendship band (with thin cross sections), string only nine beads for the beginning round.

▶ Create the band according to the instructions on page 15. Use the above patterns completely to your liking, or you can modify them.

▶ Finish the band as described on page 15.

WHAT YOU NEED:
- Native American beads
- Nylon thread
- Pair of scissors and measuring tape
- Fine sewing and bead needle

Simple Bands

Simple macramé knots and unusual materials produce interesting results. You can also attach an eye-catching ornament anywhere on, or at the ends of, the band.

Instructions

Blue Leather Bracelet

▷ Take three leather strings of about 40 inches and of different and complementary blues and tie them together at the beginning with a knot. Fasten the three strings to a surface.

▷ Begin with a short triple braid (see page 12).

▷ Then tie the actual band with square knots (as described on page 19), except here we have one string, not two, running through the center as a standing thread. The bracelet will look different on the two sides because of the two colors of the knotting threads.

▷ When the friendship band is long enough, make triple braids on both ends and then finish them off with a knot.

Green Decorative Band

▷ Pull four silk strings, three in green and one in a contrasting color, through a large bead or a brooch so that the ornament is in the middle. You can even use a wristwatch.

▷ Fasten the strings with adhesive tape and fix them to a surface so that you can comfortably knot the strings together.

▷ Create half of the band with square knots (see page 19). It will come out beautifully if you use two different colors of knotting threads. Work the other half in the same way.

▷ Finally, secure both ends with knots.

Band with Yellow Beads

▷ Tie two leather strings in contrasting colors together with a knot at about 4 inches from the beginning and fasten it to a surface.

▷ Make half-hitch chain knots (according to the instructions on page 18) until the band is long enough.

▷ Secure the knotted band with a knot and fasten beads to its ends for decoration.

Earth-tone Bands

By incorporating wooden and ceramic beads, horn buttons, and silver crosses into your friendship band you can create splendid and distinctive pieces of jewelry. The macramé knots shown here can best be tied when you fasten the beginning of the band onto a surface.

WHAT YOU NEED:
- Embroidery floss or leather strings
- Large beads made of wood, ceramic, or other materials
- Pair of scissors and measuring tape
- Adhesive tape or safety pin

Instructions

Red Leather Band

▷ Pull two leather strings about 40 inches long through a bead with a large enough hole and fold each string in half.

▷ Tie on one side a long row of half-hitch chain knots (see page 18).

▷ Complete with the other side the same way.

Spiral Band

▷ Place two leather strings about 40 inches long together. Tie them together with a knot, leaving about 4 inches on the top.

▷ Then tie with many half-hitch knots into a spiral (see page 18). The knotting thread becomes shorter.

▷ When the spiral reaches the desired length of the friendship band, string up a silver cross or a bead. Continue to make half-hitch knots now using only the *long* string as the knotting thread.

▷ Secure the end with a thick knot.

Band with Horn Button

▷ Cut eight embroidery flosses (six: 20 inches long; two: 40 inches long). For each side of the band, fold one long and three short threads in half and loop them through a horn button (or bead). The two long threads

on each side form *one* knotting thread; the six short ones become the *three* standing threads.

▷ Make one half-hitch knot with the knotting thread around each of the three standing threads (see **Fig. a** and page 18) — from the left to the right, then back again, and so on. You could make the *two* outer half-hitch knots for *one* double half-hitch knot (see pages 17–18); the technique is the same.

▷ Complete the other side in the same way and knot the ends.

Twin Band

▷ Place six embroidery flosses about 24 inches long together. Tie them with a knot, leaving about 3¼ inches at the top. Put the threads in pairs.

▷ Knot four square knots around one pair of threads (see page 19), then divide the threads into two groups and pull them through the beads.

▷ Complete the band in this manner (four square knots, two beads).

Two-colored Band

▷ Cut eight embroidery flosses of two colors into 24 inches. Place them together and tie them with 4 inches at the top. Arrange the threads in such a way that one color is in the inside and the other color is on the outside in pairs.

▷ Knot three square knots (see page 19).

▷ Divide the threads according to **Figure b**: Slip one thread of each color through a bead, knot on the outside three one-colored threads with six half-hitch or three double half-hitch knots (see pages 17–18).

▷ Repeat this method until the band is long enough. Triple-braid the ends.

Fig. a

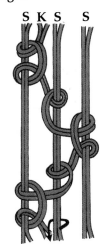

S K S   S

Fig. b

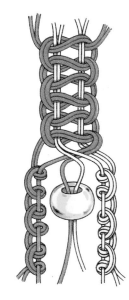

Winding Colors

Make magic with some tropical colors for your hair or wrist. These hair wraps are very quick and simple to create. Choose any colors you like for them.

Instructions

WHAT YOU NEED:
- Cotton, viscose, or Lurex threads
- Pair of scissors and measuring tape
- Beads
- Glue

Hair Wrap in Red, White, and Blue

▷ Cut one red, two blue, and three white threads to about 40 inches long. Fold them in half, leave a loop on top, and tie them together with a knot.

▷ Begin the band with the blue and white threads, using the winding technique (see page 11).

▷ Let two red and four blue threads hang out for the crosswise wrapping. Before winding this area with white, bind in four new white threads to reinforce the "core." To do this, fold four white threads (8 inches long) in half and tie them firmly below the last winding. Then wrap the area with white.

▷ For the crosswise wrapping, wind a spiral around the white threads with one red and two blue threads, then wrap the other three threads the other way round.

▷ Make a few more white and blue sections. After the final knot, make two braids.

Orange Band

▷ Use two threads in orange, one in red, and one in yellow. Fold them in half.

▷ Create the band with the winding technique, using yellow and red at the beginning (see page 11).

▷ Make the next section in orange, but first let a yellow thread hang freely

so that it can wind in a spiral afterwards over the orange.

▶ Continue the sections and then divide the threads in the end. Make two triple braids.

Four-colored Hair Wrap

▶ Using Lurex threads, choose two threads in orange and one in red, one in lilac, and one in turquoise. Fold them in half and create several one-colored sections using the winding technique (see page 11).

▶ Wrap a section in orange and then wind any of the other threads, which were hanging freely before, around it in a spiral to make a crosswise wrapping (see description of red, white, and blue wrap).

▶ For decoration, tie a bead to the end with a knot. If necessary, add some glue to make it stay.

Ring Band

▶ To make the band that is second from the right in the photo, fold in half two threads of red, turquoise, and yellow each. Use the winding technique on page 11. Make sure that you are evenly distancing the fine rings.

▶ Finish by tying on a bead with a knot. If necessary, glue it on.

Hair Wrap for Beginners

▶ The right band is the easiest one to make in this group. You need two threads in lilac, two in red, and one Lurex thread in turquoise. Fold them in half and use the winding technique (see page 11) to create sections of different lengths by using a different-colored thread each time to do the wrapping.

▶ Finally, tie on a bead with a knot. If necessary, glue it on.

Basic Diagonally Striped Patterns

Anyone who wants to make friendship bands will need to know how to make these simple diagonally-striped patterns. The patterns can be varied in many different ways, depending on the number of threads used and their colors. The examples here use light- to dark-colored threads.

Instructions

WHAT YOU NEED:
- Embroidery floss
- Pair of scissors and measuring tape
- Adhesive tape and safety pin

Green Band

The left band in the photo is created with basic knots done clockwise. The general instruction for the basic knots and the explanation of the symbols for the patterns are found on pages 16–17.

▷ Cut eight embroidery flosses about 48 inches long. Have two of each in pink, yellow, blue, and green. Tie them together with a knot, fasten the knot, and then arrange the threads according to the pattern in the first line of **Figure a**.

▷ Now follow the pattern. In step 1, use the left pink thread and make basic knots over the seven threads to the right, one after another.

▷ Then knot, in the same way, the yellow, blue, and green threads across their rows (steps 2 to 4). The rows become automatically diagonal.

▷ After step 4, the colors are back in the same sequence as in the beginning. From here, repeat steps 1–4 as often as necessary until the band is long enough.

▷ Finally, braid the ends.

Fig. a

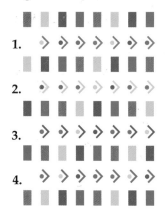

1.
2.
3.
4.

■ Pink ■ Blue
■ Yellow ■ Green

Wide Rainbow Band

The friendship band in the middle of the photo is created like the green band, but here there are more threads used and the basic knots go counter-clockwise (see page 16–17).

- Cut twelve embroidery flosses 48 inches long. Have two of each floss in lilac, blue, green, yellow, orange, and red. Tie them together with a knot, fasten the knot, and arrange the threads according to the pattern in the first line of **Figure b**.
- According to the pattern in step 1, use the right red thread and make basic knots over the eleven threads to the left, one after another. Continue the band from steps 2 to 6.
- After step 6, the colors are back in the same sequence as in the beginning. From here, repeat steps 1 to 6 until the band is long enough.
- To finish, you can either braid or twist the ends (see pages 11 and 12).

Fig. b

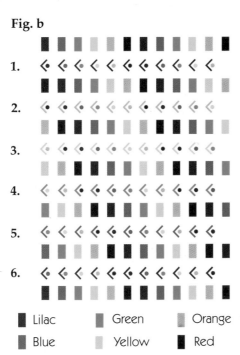

Lilac	Green	Orange
Blue	Yellow	Red

Fig.

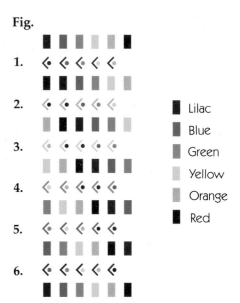

- Lilac
- Blue
- Green
- Yellow
- Orange
- Red

Narrow Rainbow Band

The band at the right of the photo is knotted in the same way as the wide rainbow band (basic knots go counter-clockwise), except that you use only half the number of threads.

- Cut six embroidery flosses about 48 inches long. Have one floss for each of these colors: lilac, blue, green, yellow, orange, and red. Tie and fasten the threads. Then arrange them according to the pattern in the first line of **Figure c**.
- According to the pattern in step 1, use the right red thread and make basic knots over the five threads to the left, one after another.
- Continue the band from steps 2 to 6. Repeats steps 1 to 6 again until the band is long enough.
- Triple-braid both ends.

Reverse Bands

These two zigzag bands are only a variation of the basic diagonally striped patterns. The trick is to turn the band several times over during the weaving process. The bands are very easy to make, despite how complicated it may look.

■ Blue
▫ Yellow
■ Red

Instructions

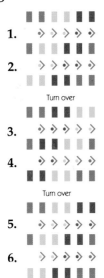

WHAT YOU NEED:
- Embroidery floss
- Pair of scissors and measuring tape
- Adhesive tape and safety pin

Fig. a

Narrow Multicolored Band

This band is made only with basic knots done clockwise (see page 16).

▶ Cut six embroidery flosses about 48 inches long. Have two of each in blue, yellow, and red. Tie and fasten them. Arrange the threads according to the pattern in the first line of **Figure a.**

▶ According to the pattern in step 1, use the first left blue thread and make basic knots over the five threads to the right, one after another. Do the same with the second blue thread in step 2.

▶ Now turn the piece over so that you begin again with two blue threads. Knot these two blue rows and again turn everything over. Finally, knot these two blue rows for the third time (steps 3 to 6).

▶ Without reversing back to the blue threads, continue steps 7 to 12 by using and reversing back to the two yellow threads.

▶ Without reversing, begin step 13 with the red threads and continue to step 18.

▶ Repeat these steps as long as necessary until the band is long enough.

▶ To finish, braid both ends.

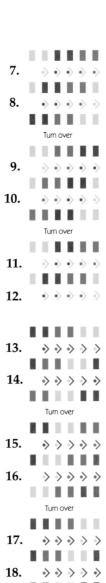

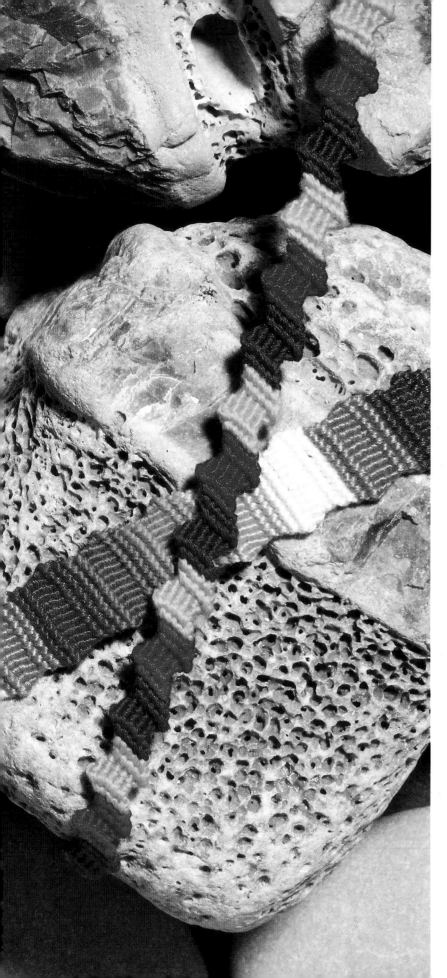

Wide Green Band

This variation is made in the same manner as the narrow multicolored band except that the basic knots are done counterclockwise. This band also uses more numbers of threads.

▷ Cut twelve embroidery flosses 48 inches long. Have two of each floss in dark, medium, and light green as well as in light, medium, and dark blue. Tie and fasten them. Then arrange the threads according to the pattern in the first line of **Figure b**.

▷ Now work like the narrow multicolored band, except begin at the right. Create two rows of dark blue with basic knots done counterclockwise, turn the piece over, knot two rows again, turn over, and knot two rows for the third time (steps 1 to 6).

▷ After these six rows in dark blue, *without* reversing, begin with the two medium blue threads and continue working in this same manner.

▷ When the band is long enough, braid both ends.

Fig. b

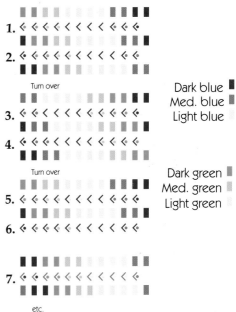

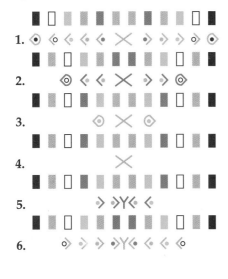

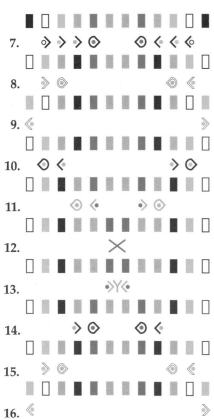

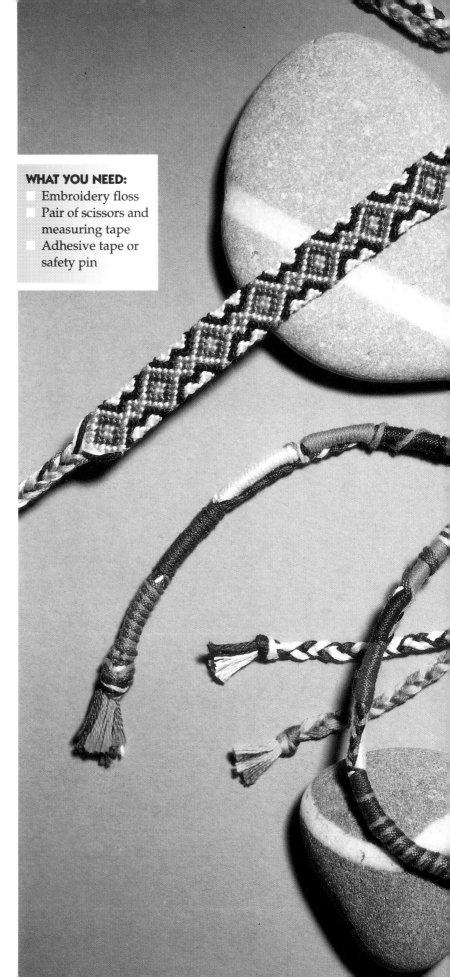

Wound and Knotted Bands

Hair wraps and knotted friendship bands can be made with any colors. If you already know how to wind hair wraps, here are some brief ideas on how to create variations.

Instructions

Winding Patterns for Hair Wraps

The hair wraps shown in the photo are made from the winding technique according to the instructions on page 11. You can, of course, experiment with these following patterns.

- *One-colored sections:* Take one thread from the strand and wrap it around all the others.
- *Simple spiral:* Take two different threads out of the strand. Wrap the section in one color with one of the strands. Then take the second strand and wind it in a spiral around the section.
- *Crosswise winding:* Take three threads out of the strand. Wrap the section in one, wind into a spiral with the second (see above), and wind the third in a spiral going in the opposite direction of the second thread.
- *Ring spiral:* Use two or three different-colored threads and wind them at the same time tightly around the strand. This way, you do not need to wrap the section beforehand with just one color.
- *Mini-braids:* Let four threads (for one braid) or seven threads (for two braids) hang out of the strand. First wrap this section with one thread in one color. Braid the other three (or six) threads and use the braid to decorate over the section.

Large and Small Diamonds

This band is made with basic and double half-hitch knots. The general instruction and the symbol explanations for the pattern in **Figure a** are on pages 16–17. The light green threads do not become visible in the band.

- Cut twelve embroidery flosses about 48 inches long. Have two of each floss in pink, blue, orange, white, black, and light green. Tie the threads together with a knot and fasten it. Then arrange the threads according to pattern in the first line of **Figure a**.
- *Large diamond:* In step 1, tie the two threads in the middle together with a knot, then tie them to the next four threads at the left and at the right with basic knots, and finish with one double half-hitch knot at both sides. Steps 1, 2, and 3 are done knotting outward; steps 5 and 6 are done inward.
- *Small diamond:* Steps 7 to 17 cover the small squares in the band. Follow the directions of the arrows of the steps as to whether you should knot outward or inward.
- In the end, the threads are back in the same sequence as in the beginning. Start again and repeat these steps as often as necessary until the band is long enough.
- Decorate the ends with braids.

Arrowheads and Crisscrosses

You can make these arrowhead bands in the same way as the diagonally striped bands, except that you need to knot from the center, not the edge. The arrows will come out pointing in one direction. Both bands in the photo are based on this principle.

Instructions

WHAT YOU NEED:
- Embroidery floss
- Pair of scissors and measuring tape
- Adhesive tape or safety pin

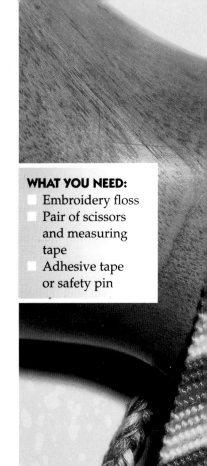

Multicolored Arrowheads

For this colorful band, you only need to make the basic knots in a clockwise and counterclockwise fashion. The general instructions for these knots as well as the explanation for the symbols in the patterns are on pages 16–17.

▸ Cut sixteen embroidery flosses about 48 inches long. Have four of each floss in blue, yellow, pink, and orange. Tie the threads together with a knot and fasten them. Now arrange the threads symmetrically by following the sequence in step 1 of **Figure a**.

▸ Tie the two pink threads in the middle together with a knot. Then tie them to the eight threads to the left and to the right with basic knots (step 1).

▸ Steps 2 to 8 bring each color once from the center outward.

▸ After step 8, the colors are back in the same sequence as in the beginning. Repeat these steps until the band is as long as you like.

▸ Braid the beginning and end pieces to finish the band.

Diamonds with Crisscrosses

This band consists of basic and double half-hitch knots that are done to the right and to the left (see pages 16–17).

▸ Cut twelve embroidery flosses about 48 inches long. Have two of each floss in lilac, blue, green, white, orange, and pink. Tie the threads together with a knot and fasten them. Then arrange the threads symmetrically according to the pattern in the first line of **Figure b**.

▸ *Diamond:* In step 1, tie the threads in the center together with a knot. Then tie them to the five threads to the left and right of them by using four basic knots and one double half-hitch knot.

▸ Now continue with the orange and white threads from the inside to the outside, and complete the diamond by reversing rows from the outside to the inside (steps 2 to 6).

▸ *Crisscross:* Steps 7 to 12 form the lilac crisscrosses and the corners. Follow these steps whether knotting inward or outward.

▸ After step 12, the colors are back in the same sequence as in the beginning. Repeat steps 1 to 12 until the band is as long as you like.

▸ Braiding two colorful pairs of cords completes the band.

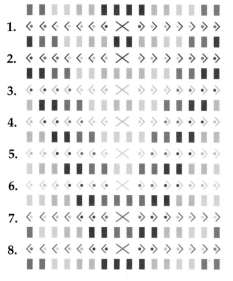

Fig. a

1. ‹ ‹ ‹ ‹ ‹ ‹ ✕ › › › › › ›
2. ‹ ‹ ‹ ‹ ‹ ‹ ✕ › › › › › ›
3. ‹ ‹ ‹ ‹ ‹ ‹ ✕ › › › › › ›
4. ‹ ‹ ‹ ‹ ‹ ✕ › › › › › ›
5. ‹ ‹ ‹ ‹ ‹ ✕ › › › › › ›
6. ‹ ‹ ‹ ‹ ‹ ✕ › › › › ›
7. ‹ ‹ ‹ ‹ ‹ ‹ ✕ › › › › › ›
8. ‹ ‹ ‹ ‹ ‹ ‹ ✕ › › › › › ›

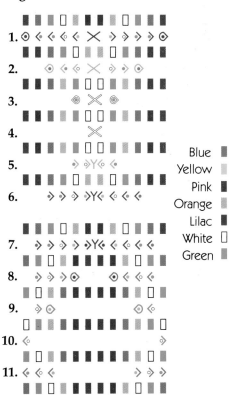

Fig. b

1. ⊙ ‹ ‹ ‹ ‹ ‹ ✕ › › › › ⊙
2. ⊙ ‹ ‹ ⊙ ✕ › ⊙ › ⊙
3. ◉ ✕ ◉
4. ✕
5. › ›Y‹ ‹
6. › › › ›Y‹ ‹ ‹ ‹
7. › › › › ›Y‹ ‹ ‹ ‹ ‹
8. › › › ⊙ ⊙ ‹ ‹ ‹
9. › ⊙ ◉ ⊙ ‹
10. ‹ ›
11. ‹ ‹ › › ›
12. ‹ ‹ ‹ ‹ ‹ › › › › › ›

Blue ■
Yellow ■
Pink ■
Orange ■
Lilac ■
White □
Green ■

55

Changing-direction Bands

The classic arrowhead pattern points in one direction. The other band shown in the photo has striped triangles jumping up and down. Both bands can be easily made.

Instructions

Arrowhead Pattern

Basic knots, done clockwise and counterclockwise, are all you need to make this band. The instruction for making basic knots and the explanation of the symbols in the pattern are on pages 16–17.

▶ Cut twelve flosses 48 inches long. Have two of each floss in lilac, dark red, white, and yellow, and four flosses in black. Tie the threads together with a knot and fasten them. Then arrange the threads symmetrically according to the pattern in the first line of **Figure a**.

Fig. a

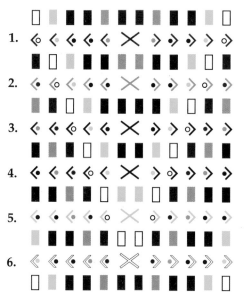

- ☐ White
- ◼ Black
- ◼ Dark red
- ▨ Lilac
- ▨ Yellow

- Follow the pattern. In step 1, tie the red threads in the middle together with a knot, then tie them to each of the five threads to the left and right of them using a basic knot.
- Steps 2 to 6 continue this pattern until all colors move once from the inside to the outside.
- After step 6, all colors are back in the same sequence as in the beginning. Repeat steps 1 to 6 until the band is long enough.
- Finish the ends with two braids.

Dancing Triangles

This pattern may look complicated, but it consists of only basic knots done clockwise or counterclockwise.

- Cut nine embroidery flosses about 48 inches long. Have one floss in white, two in green and yellow each, and four in dark red. Tie them together with a knot and then fasten them. Arrange the threads according to the pattern in the first line of **Figure b**.
- *Left triangle:* Work the left triangles with clockwise basic knots. In steps 1 to 8, Begin each row on the left side and make one knot less from row to row.
- *Right triangle:* Work the right triangles in the same way, with counterclockwise basic knots. In steps 9 to 16, begin each row on the right side and make one less knot from row to row.
- After step 16, the colors are back in the same sequence as in the beginning. Continue steps 1 to 16 until the band is long enough.
- To finish, braid both sides.

Fig. b

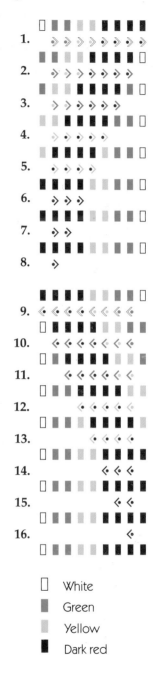

Combination Patterns

This symmetrically constructed band has four patterns. These patterns can be done in different sizes and color combinations. You can combine the patterns in your own way. More experienced friendship band-makers should have no problem creating this band.

Instructions

Pattern Variations

Basic and double half-hitch knots are used for this band in the photo. Instructions for these knots as well as symbol explanations are on pages 16–17. These four patterns can be combined as often as you like.

▶ Cut twelve embroidery flosses about 48 inches long. Have two of each

Fig. a: Small Diamonds

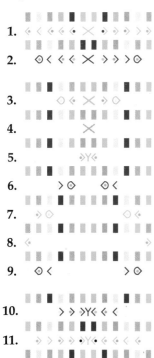

floss in lilac, creme, gray, light green, dark blue, and yellow. Tie the threads togethers with a knot and fasten them. Arrange the threads according to the pattern in the first line of **Figure a**.

▶ *Row of small diamonds:* The band contains rows of two to five little diamonds in completely different color combinations. To start, knot one yellow and one blue row with basic knots. Begin, in each case, in the middle and work to the left and to the right (steps 1 and 2). Then knot the first green small diamond (steps 3 to 9). For more small diamonds, repeat steps 3 to 9, but leave out the *middle knot* in step 3. In order to close the row, substitute *in the last repetition* steps 10 to 11 for steps 6 to 9.

▶ *Arrowheads, pointing downward:* Below the first row of small diamonds are three arrowheads pointing downward **(Fig. b)**. To make these arrowheads, knot in each row basic knots going from the outside to the inside (steps 1 to 3).

▶ *Triangles:* Below the arrowheads are two triangles standing opposite each other. They are made according to steps 1 to 4 in **Figure c.**

▶ Next in the band are two small squares, one green arrowhead pointing downward, and two triangles. To make them, follow the instructions above.

▷ *Arrowheads, pointing upward:* The three arrowheads following in the band are now pointing upward. They are knotted according to steps 1 to 3 in **Figure d**.

▷ Continue the band with these four patterns as often as you like until the band is long enough. Vary the number of the arrowheads just as you should vary the length of the rows of the small diamonds, so that the band looks lively with alternating colors.

▷ Complete the band with two braids.

▮ Lilac	▮ Light green
▮ White	▮ Dark violet
▮ Gray	▮ Yellow

Fig. b: Downward Arrowheads

Fig. c: Triangles

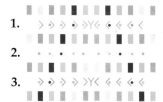

Fig. d: Upward Arrowheads

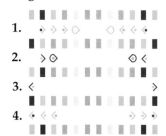

Step Patterns

These patterns are a lot of fun for the experienced friendship band-maker once you are used to the design.

Instructions

Multicolored Band

This band, shown in the photo resting beneath the green band, consists of basic and double half-hitch knots. The instructions for the knots as well as an explanation for pattern symbols are on pages 16–17.

▸ Cut eighteen embroidery flosses. Have two of each in dark red, light green, dark green, orange, medium yellow, light yellow, and dark violet, as well as four in medium violet. Tie the threads together with a knot and fasten them. Arrange the threads according to the pattern in the first line of **Figure a**.

▸ *Beginning:* Knot three rows out of the center (steps 1 to 3).

▸ *Pattern:* For steps 4 and 5, start from the center. Then knot on both sides, as indicated, two knots towards the center (i.e., steps 6 to 9 starts, respectively, from the 8th, 6th, 4th, and 2nd positions from the sides). For steps 10 to 14, make the knots with the threads in the odd-numbered positions: from the 1st, 3rd, 7th, and 9th positions towards the outside.

▸ From here on, repeat steps 4 to 14 **(Fig. b)**.

▸ Now repeat steps 4 to 14 about twenty times. Pay attention to the positions no matter which colors you are dealing with in each step.

▸ Finish with a pair of braids.

Fig. a

(Pattern chart with columns numbered 1 2 3 4 5 6 7 8 9 9 8 7 6 5 4 3 2 1 and rows numbered 1. through 14.)

WHAT YOU NEED:
- Embroidery floss
- Pair of scissors and measuring tape
- Adhesive tape or safety pin

Green Variation

The green band in the photo shows how different the same pattern can look when you use different color combinations.

Fig. b

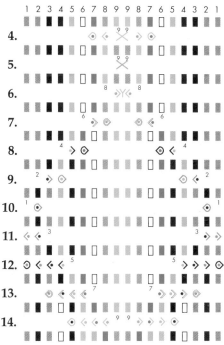

■ Dark red

■ Dark green

■ Light green

■ Orange

■ Medium yellow

□ Light yellow

■ Dark violet

■ Medium lilac

Square Pattern

The band in this photo has an exquisite look from the combination of basic square patterns with the centerpiece knotted in stripes. A couple of buttons are used for decoration.

Instructions

Diamond Band with Basic Colors

This basic pattern is created by rows of diamonds separated by black lines. One row contains solid-colored diamonds. Another contains two-colored diamonds in which the red points upward or downward. The stripe patterns in the middle are especially easily knotted. Only basic and double half-hitch knots (done clockwise and counterclockwise) are needed. Instructions for the knots as well as the pattern symbols are on pages 16–17.

▶ Cut eighteen embroidery flosses about 48 inches long. Have four of each floss in yellow, red, and blue, as well as six in black. Arrange the threads according to the first line of **Figure a**. It is best to glue the beginning piece at about 4 inches long to a surface.

▶ *Beginning row:* Knot the black threads at the three areas of step 1 in **Figure a**.

▶ *One-colored small squares:* Follow steps 2 to 4 of **Figure a** to make one row of small squares in yellow, red, and blue that are separated by black lines.

▶ *Two-colored small squares with red pointing downward:* For the next row with small squares made of two colors follow steps 1 to 4 of **Figure b**.

▶ To make another row of one-colored small squares, simply repeat steps 2 to 4 of **Figure a**.

▶ *Two-colored small squares with red pointing upward:* To make this row, follow steps 1 to 4 of **Figure c**.

▶ Continue in the band by alternating the steps of the Figures: a (always only steps 2 to 4), b, a, c, a, b, a, c, and so on. Before making the center stripes, finish with one row of one-colored small squares **(Fig. a)**.

▶ *Transition steps:* Before the middle of the band, follow the steps 1 and 2 of **Figure d**, then divide the threads into four groups as shown in step 3.

▶ *Striped bands:* Knot the four groups independently of one another by following steps 1 to 3 of **Figures e, f, g**, and **h**. You'll have small, narrow bands in the diagonally striped patterns. The three steps of each figure can be repeated as many times as you like.

▶ Pull the small bands in the middle crosswise through the hole of the wooden button. Then pull both through a blue bead and again, as above, through the wooden button.

▶ *Transition steps:* Arrange the threads according to the first line in **Figure i**. Work steps 1 and 2.

▶ Now create the second half of the band again, following the basic patterns in **Figures a, b**, and **c**.

▶ To finish the band, string a bead onto the two threads in the middle at both ends and make two pairs of braids.

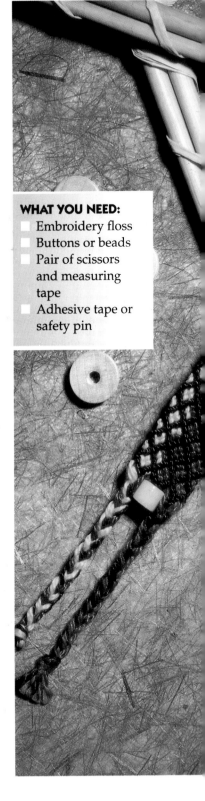

WHAT YOU NEED:
- Embroidery floss
- Buttons or beads
- Pair of scissors and measuring tape
- Adhesive tape or safety pin

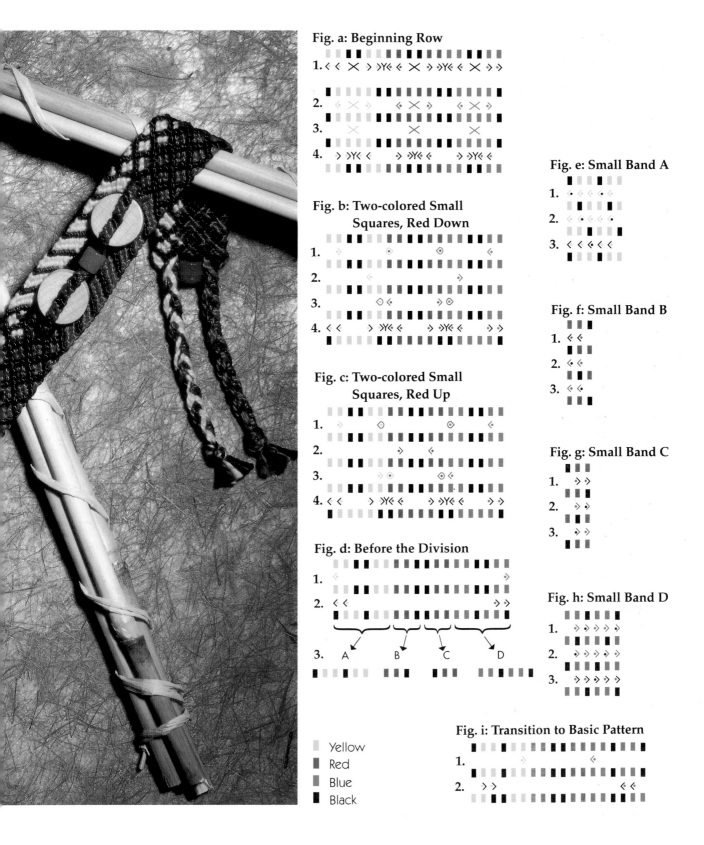

Fig. a: Beginning Row

Fig. b: Two-colored Small Squares, Red Down

Fig. c: Two-colored Small Squares, Red Up

Fig. d: Before the Division

Fig. e: Small Band A

Fig. f: Small Band B

Fig. g: Small Band C

Fig. h: Small Band D

Fig. i: Transition to Basic Pattern

Yellow
Red
Blue
Black

INDEX